Cicciolina

Photos Riccardo Schicchi

Cicciolina

Ilona Staller

Benedikt Taschen

© 1992 Benedikt Taschen Verlag GmbH
Hohenzollernring 53, D-5000 Köln 1
© Ilona Staller
Edited by Angelika Muthesius, Köln
Deutsche Übersetzung: Britta Behnke, Bonn
English translation: John Smith, Cologne
Traduction française: Michèle Schreyer, Cologne
Reproductions: Krefting & Melcher, Düsseldorf
Typesetting: Utesch Satztechnik GmbH, Hamburg
Printed in Germany
ISBN 3-8228-9761-2

Cicciolina, sono io

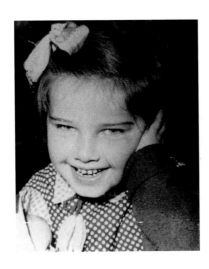

Io con cinque anni

Sono nata a Budapest, mio padre era funzionario del Ministero degli Interni e mia madre faceva l'ostetrica. La mia carriera di fotomodella è cominciata molto presto: già all'età di tredici anni posavo per un'agenzia fotografica di Budapest, la MTI, per la quale lavoravano allora le cinquanta migliori fotomodelle ungheresi. Da bambina sognavo di diventare archeologa e così, dopo essermi iscritta all'università e aver cominciato a studiare medicina, decisi di dedicarmi all'archeologia.

Veramente famosa sono diventata in Italia, con una trasmissione radiofonica, Radio Luna, che riscosse grandissimo successo. Fu allora che inventai il mio nome d'arte, Cicciolina.

Era il 1976: allestimmo una tournée di shows musicali che presentammo nelle più grandi discoteche italiane. Io posavo nuda, tra colombe e serpenti vivi, dentro una bolla di plexiglas, sullo sfondo di scenografie dai colori sgargianti. Cantavo dolcemente le mie canzoni con le quali cominciavo a provocare quel comune senso del pudore cui tanto teneva l'Italia!

Un successo e una risonanza ancor più grandi li riscossi con uno spettacolo televisivo in sei puntate, «C'era due volte», realizzato nel 1978 con la regia di Enzo Trapani. Io, Cicciolina, osavo mostrare il mio seno nudo su una rete nazionale! Ci fu uno scandalo incredibile! Eppure a quello seguirono molti altri spettacoli, interviste, inviti alla televisione; intanto giravo anche film erotico-pornografici.

Nel 1979, grazie alla mia fama e al mio atteggiamento provocante, fui scelta quale capolista della «Lista del Sole», il primo partito verde italiano. Cominciò così il mio impegno politico: lavoravo attivamente per la raccolta delle firme a favore dei referendum proposti dal partito radicale, al quale mi iscrissi nel 1985, partecipavo alle manifestazioni contro l'energia nucleare, per il rispetto dei diritti umani, contro la fame nel mondo. Nei miei spettacoli si fece strada la politica e, ahimè, ecco arrivare le prime denunce. Né io né i miei elettori ci lasciammo scoraggiare: il ciclone Cicciolina non si ferma!

Quando, nel 1987, mi candidai per il partito radicale, la mia circoscrizione elettorale mi premiò con ben 20 000 preferenze. Per la prima volta nella storia politica dell'Italia una pornodiva veniva eletta al parlamento! I miei obiettivi politici sono chiari: io sono per

«Radio Luna», 1976

5

« Radio Luna», 1976   Con la mia mamma Ilona

un futuro sicuro senza energia nucleare, sono per l'assoluta libertà sessuale, per il diritto all'amore anche nelle carceri, per l'educazione sessuale nelle scuole, per una corretta informazione riguardo all'AIDS, contro ogni forma di censura e contro la pena di morte, contro ogni forma di violenza e per la regolamentazione della droga. E tutto questo senza perdere mai di vista l'amore! L'amore per la natura, per esempio, che mi induce a proporre una tassa ecologica con la quale limitare l'inquinamento e a lottare contro lo sterminio degli animali e contro la vivisezione.

L'impegno politico, comunque, non mi allontana dal mio pubblico che continua a richiedere la mia presenza e la mia spontaneità. Cantando «Living in the paradise» canto, sì, a nome del mondo intero!

Nel 1990 l'artista americano Jeff Koons mi ha dedicato una sua opera che è stata presentata con grande successo alla Biennale di Venezia. Da deputatessa sono diventata opera d'arte! Il primo giugno del 1991 Jeff Koons, cittadino americano, ha sposato Ilona Staller, la ragazza dell'Est. Eppure io, sua moglie, non lo posso raggiungere negli Stati Uniti: oggi, nel 1992, le autorità americane si rifiutano di concedermi un visto d'entrata. Per le strade di New York, però, si vede un grande cartellone, una finestra aperta sul paradiso, realizzato da mio marito, che annuncia a tutta l'America la nostra felicità. «Nostro figlio», dice Jeff, «sarà la mia più grande opera d'arte, il nostro futuro, la nostra reincarnazione. Lui ci renderà eterni.»

Vi amo
Ilona Staller
Cicciolina

Cicciolina, das bin ich

Mein kleiner Bruder Attila

Geboren wurde ich in Budapest als Tochter eines Beamten des Innenministeriums und einer Hebamme. Meine Karriere als Fotomodell hat früh begonnen: Bereits im Alter von 13 Jahren stand ich Modell für die Agentur MTI, welche die fünfzig besten Modelle Ungarns unter Vertrag hatte. Schon als Kind träumte ich davon, Archäologin zu werden, und so entschied ich mich – nachdem ich mich bereits an der Universität für Medizin eingeschrieben und zu studieren begonnen hatte –, mich dennoch der Archäologie zuzuwenden.

Wirklich berühmt bin ich in Italien mit der Radiosendung »Radio Luna« geworden, die ein riesiger Erfolg war. Für diese Sendung legte ich mir den Künstlernamen »Cicciolina« zu.

Im Jahre 1976 hatte ich meine ersten größeren Live-Auftritte. Wir tourten durch die bekanntesten Diskotheken des Landes. So saß ich etwa – nackt, vor einem bunten Bühnenbild – in einer großen Seifenblase aus Plexiglas zwischen Tauben und lebenden Schlangen und hauchte mit sanfter Stimme meine Lieder ins Mikrofon. Damit begann ich, das damalige allgemeine Schamgefühl in Italien zu provozieren!

Noch größere Resonanz hatte einer meiner ersten Auftritte im Fernsehen 1978. In der Show »C'era due volte«, unter der Regie von Enzo Trapani, gab es eine Premiere: Mein nackter Busen war die erste entblößte Brust, die im italienischen Fernsehen zu sehen war, was zu dieser Zeit einen Skandal auslöste. Viele andere Auftritte, Interviews, Fernsehsendungen und Pornofilme folgten.

Aufgrund meiner Berühmtheit und meiner provozierenden Haltung wurde ich 1979 zur Spitzenkandidatin der »Lista del Sole«, der ersten grünen Partei Italiens, gewählt. Außerdem machte ich mich bei öffentlichen Auftritten für die »Partito Radicale«, bei der ich mich 1985 einschrieb, stark, um mich gegen Atomenergie, für die Wahrung der Menschenrechte sowie gegen den Hunger in der Welt einzusetzen. Auf meine Auftritte folgten die ersten Strafanzeigen, was jedoch meine Wähler nicht davon abhielt, bei den Wahlen für mich mit Ja zu stimmen. Der Wirbelsturm »Cicciolina« war nicht mehr zu bremsen.

Im Jahre 1987 wurde ich mit 20 000 Stimmen von meinem Wahlkreis Roma-Lazio ins italienische Parlament gewählt. Ich war der erste Pornostar, der in die Politik einzog!

Mein erster Auftritt

Während meiner Auftritte in den Shows »Piramide« (1979) und »C'era due volte«, RAI 2 TV (1978)

Meine politischen Ziele sind einfach: Ich bin für eine sichere Zukunft ohne Atomkraft, für die absolute sexuelle Freiheit, für das Recht auf Liebe in den Gefängnissen, gegen die Todesstrafe, gegen jegliche Form von Gewalt sowie für die Reglementierung der Drogen. Ich bin gegen jede Art von Zensur, für die Sexualerziehung in den Schulen und für eine sachliche Information über AIDS. Und all das, ohne die Liebe aus den Augen zu verlieren!

1990 widmete mir der amerikanische Künstler Jeff Koons eines seiner Werke, das 1990 auf der Biennale in Venedig mit großem Erfolg ausgestellt wurde. Die Abgeordnete Ilona Staller ist so zu einem Meisterwerk der Kunst geworden.

Am 1. Juni 1990 heiratete Jeff Koons, amerikanischer Staatsbürger, Ilona Staller, das Mädchen aus dem Osten. Jedoch kann ich, seine Frau, nicht in die Vereinigten Staaten einreisen: Bis heute, im Jahre 1992, weigert sich die amerikanische Einreisebehörde, mir ein Visum zu geben. Bis dahin bleibt mir nur das große Plakat mit einem Bild von Jeff und mir, das, aufgestellt in New York, Amerika unser Glück verkündet. Unsere Ehe ist ein Paradies oder wie Jeff sagt: »Unser zukünftiges Kind ist mein bestes Kunstwerk, es ist unsere Wiedergeburt, und wir werden durch das Kind unsterblich sein.«

Vi amo
Ilona Staller
Cicciolina

Cicciolina, that's me

At the beginning of my career

I was born in Budapest. My father was an official in the Ministry of the Interior, my mother a midwife. My career as a model began early; at the age of thirteen I was already working for the MTI modelling agency, which had the fifty best models in Hungary under contract.

Even as a child I dreamed of becoming an archaeologist and so – having already enrolled at university and started studying medicine – I decided to devote myself to archaeology.

In Italy I really achieved fame with a radio show called »Radio Luna«, which was a huge success. It was for that programme that I adopted the name »Cicciolina«. In 1976 I did my first major live appearances. We toured the country's top discos. I performed naked in front of a colourful stage set – sitting in a large perspex bubble, say, with doves and live snakes, breathing songs into the mike in a soft voice. And so I began provoking Italy's sensibilities!

One of my first television appearances in 1978 sparked off an even bigger response. On Enzo Trapani's show »C'era due volte« my breasts were the first to be seen bared on Italian TV. At that time it caused a scandal. Many more appearances, interviews, TV shows and porno films were to follow.

In 1979, on the strength of my fame and my provocative stance, I was elected the leading candidate of the »Lista del Sole«, Italy's first green party. After joining the »Partito Radicale« in 1985, I also used public appearances to campaign against nuclear energy, for human rights, and against starvation anywhere in the world. These appearances prompted the public prosecutor to bring charges against me, but that didn't stop my supporters giving me their votes. The »Cicciolina« whirlwind was unstoppable now.

In 1987 I polled 20,000 votes in my constituency of Lazio (Rome) and so became a member of parliament. I was the first porn star to enter politics!

My political aims are simple ones: I am for a safe future without nuclear energy, for absolute sexual freedom, for the right to sex in prisons, against the death penalty, against all forms of violence, and for the decriminalization of drugs. I am against censorship of any kind, in

»Il Partito del Sole«

During my appearances in the shows »Piramide« (1979) and »C'era due volte«, RAI 2 TV (1978)

favour of sex education in schools, and for objective information about AIDS. And all this without losing sight of love!

In 1990 the American artist Jeff Koons dedicated a work to me. It was exhibited at the 1990 Venice Biennale and was acclaimed. So Ilona Staller the member of parliament became a masterpiece of art.

On 1 June 1990 Jeff Koons, citizen of the United States, married Ilona Staller, the girl from the East. And although his wife, I am forbidden entry to the United States. Now it is 1992, and the American immigration authorities still refuse to grant me a visa. In the meantime a huge poster showing Jeff and me is on display in New York, telling America how happy we are. Our marriage is paradise. Or, as Jeff puts it: »Our future child will be my best work of art. In it we shall be reborn. Through that child we shall be immortal.«

With my husband, the American artist Jeff Koons

Vi amo
Ilona Staller
Cicciolina

10

Cicciolina, c'est moi

Photo pour ma campagne électorale par Gianfranco Salis

Je suis née à Budapest, mon père était fonctionnaire au Ministère de l'Intérieur et ma mère sage-femme. J'ai commencé très tôt ma carrière de mannequin, puisqu'à treize ans je posais déjà pour l'agence MTI, qui avait passé un contrat avec les cinquante meilleurs mannequins de Hongrie. Enfant, je rêvais de devenir archéologue, et me décidai donc – bien que j'aie déjà commencé à étudier la médecine – à me vouer à l'archéologie.

C'est en Italie que je suis vraiment devenue célèbre avec l'émission «Radio Luna», qui eut un succès prodigieux. J'ai alors adopté le nom de «Cicciolina».

Mes premières apparitions publiques datent de 1976. Nous faisions la tournée des discothèques les plus connues du pays. Il m'arrivait par exemple d'être assise – nue devant des décors multicolores – dans une grosse bulle de plexiglas au milieu de pigeons et de serpents et de murmurer doucement mes chansons dans le micro. Et c'est ainsi que j'ai commencé à défier les Italiens si pudiques à l'époque!

L'une de mes premières apparitions à la télévision en 1978 a eu encore plus de retentissement. Dans le spectacle «C'era due volte», réalisé par Enzo Trapani, on voyait pour la première fois une poitrine nue, la mienne, sur les écrans italiens. A l'époque cela a fait scandale. De nombreuses autres sorties, des interviews, des émissions télévisées et des films porno devaient suivre.

Parmi les «Marines» américains

En raison de ma célébrité et de mon attitude provocante, je suis devenue en 1979 la candidate de la «Lista del Sole», le premier parti écologique italien. En outre, j'ai soutenu publiquement dès 1985 le «Partito Radicale» en prenant parti contre l'énergie nucléaire, pour la protection des droits de l'homme ainsi qu'en protestant contre la faim dans le monde. Les premières plaintes furent déposées suite à ces activités, ce qui n'empêcha pas les gens de voter pour moi. Impossible de freiner la tornade «Cicciolina».

En 1987, je fus élue députée au Parlement italien par 20 000 voix de ma circonscription électorale de Roma-Lazo. J'étais la première vedette porno à faire de la politique!

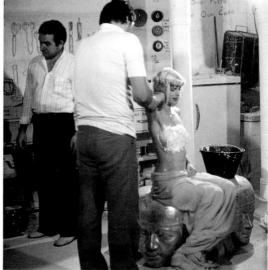

Lors du spectacle «Nel giardino dell fantasia»   Travail sur le moulage de ma poitrine

Mes objectifs politiques sont simples: je suis pour un avenir sûr sans énergie nucléaire, je suis pour la liberté sexuelle absolue, pour le droit des prisonniers à l'amour, je suis contre la peine de mort, contre toute forme de violence ainsi que pour la réglementation de la drogue. Je suis contre toute forme de censure, pour l'éducation sexuelle à l'école et pour une information objective sur le SIDA. Et tout cela sans oublier l'amour! En 1990, l'artiste américain Jeff Koons m'a consacré l'une de ses œuvres qui fut exposée la même année à la Biennale de Venise et connut un grand succès. Ilona Staller, députée, est devenue un chef-d'œuvre artistique.

Et la petite Hongroise a épousé le citoyen américain le 1er juin 1990. Mais bien qu'étant sa femme, je ne peux entrer aux Etats-Unis, vu que je n'ai toujours pas obtenu de visa jusqu'à ce jour. En attendant, il ne me reste qu'une affiche nous représentant Jeff et moi, elle est exposée à New York et témoigne de notre bonheur. Notre vie commune est un paradis, ou, comme le dit Jeff: «Notre futur enfant est mon œuvre la plus réussie, il est notre réincarnation, et nous serons immortels grâce à lui».

*Vi amo
Ilona Staller
Cicciolina*

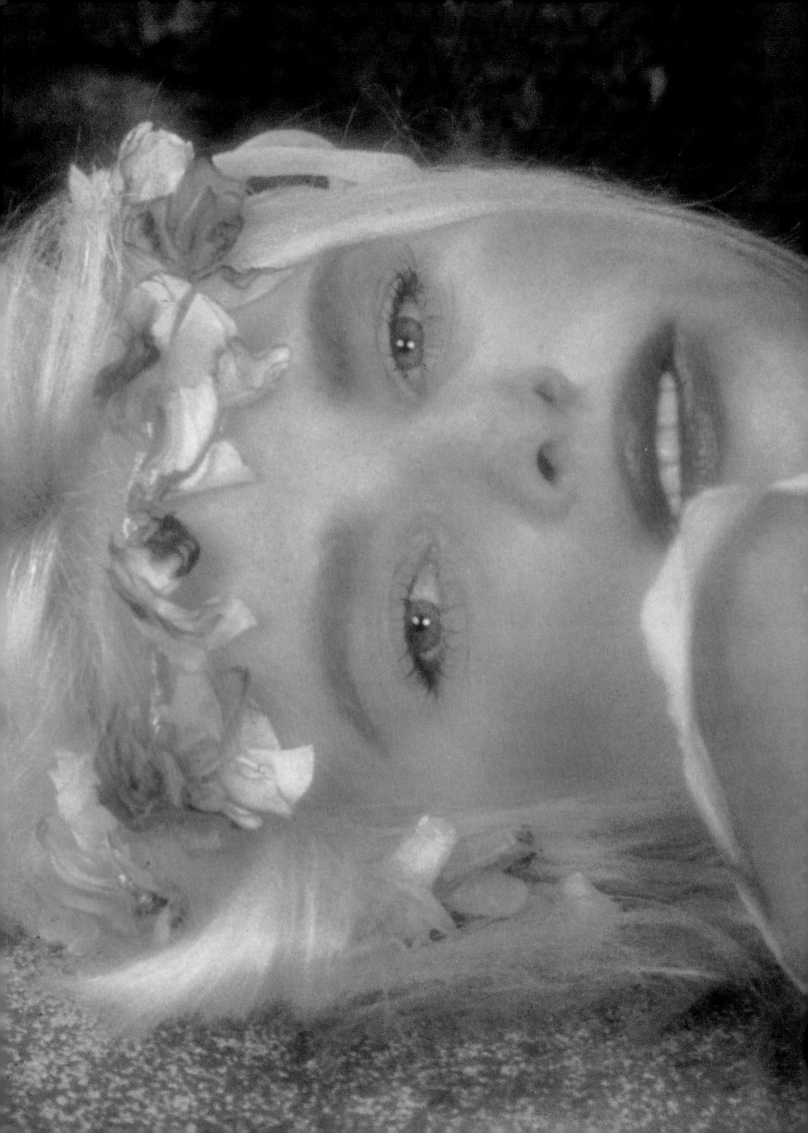

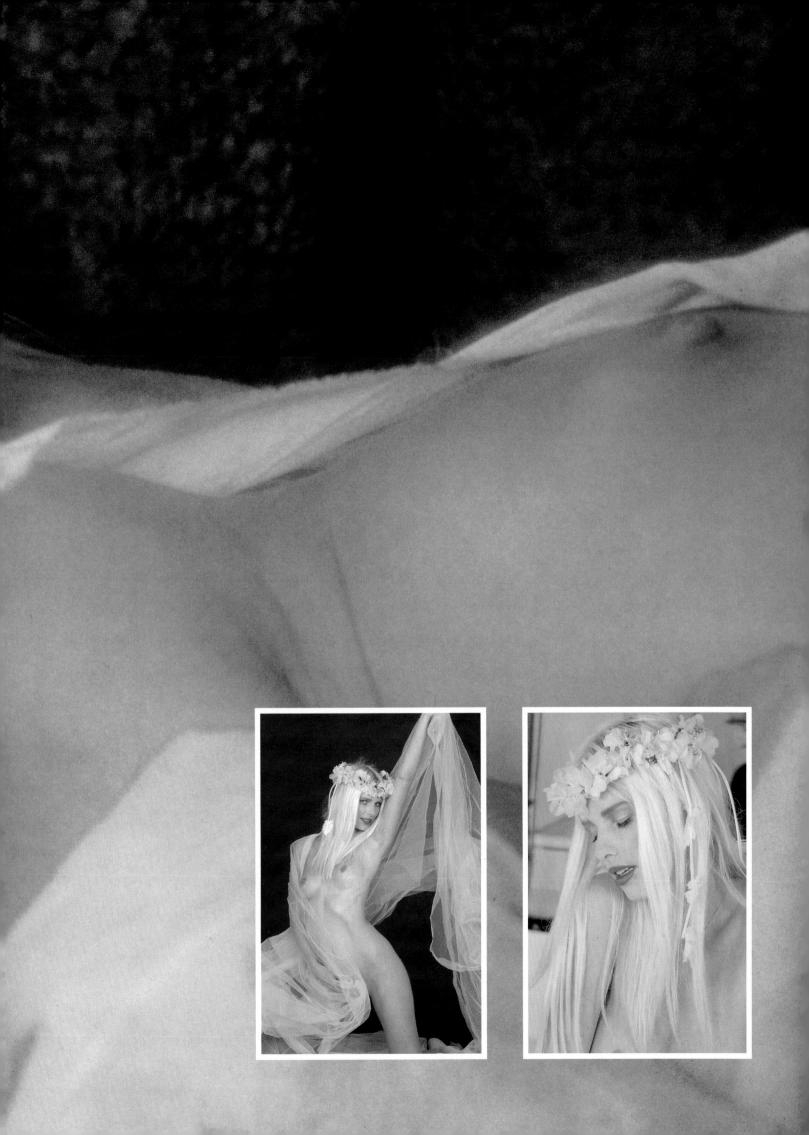

L'erotismo è un grande universo, dove vedi il cielo, le stelle, il mare trasparente.
È un sogno per chi sa sognare intensamente, perché i sogni ti si attaccano...
Erotico è il senso della vita, uno sguardo, una mano, una carezza! Ci si eccita sull'odore, sul sudore – sulle labbra.
Bisogna essere capaci di trasmettersi l'erotismo.

Die Erotik ist ein großes Universum, in dem du den Himmel, die Sterne, das klare Meer erblickst.
Ein Traum – für den, der wirklich träumen kann, denn die Träume klammern sich an dich...
Erotik ist der Sinn des Lebens, ein Blick, eine Hand – eine Liebkosung! Wie erregend ist der Geruch, der Schweiß – auf den Lippen.
Man muß dazu fähig sein, Erotik zu übertragen.

Eroticism is a wide universe where you glimpse heaven, the stars and the deep, blue sea.
A dream – for those who can really dream, for dreams cling to you...
Eroticism is the meaning of life, a look, a hand – a caress! How exciting the scent, the sweat – on lips.
You must be able to communicate eroticism.

L'érotisme est un immense univers, dans lequel tu découvres les cieux, les étoiles et les eaux limpides des mers.
C'est un rêve – pour celui qui sait vraiment rêver, car les rêves tissent leur toile autour de toi...
L'érotisme est le sens de la vie, un regard, une main – une caresse! L'odeur, la sueur – sur les lèvres – quel enivrement.
Communiquer l'érotisme est un don inné.

Cicciolina

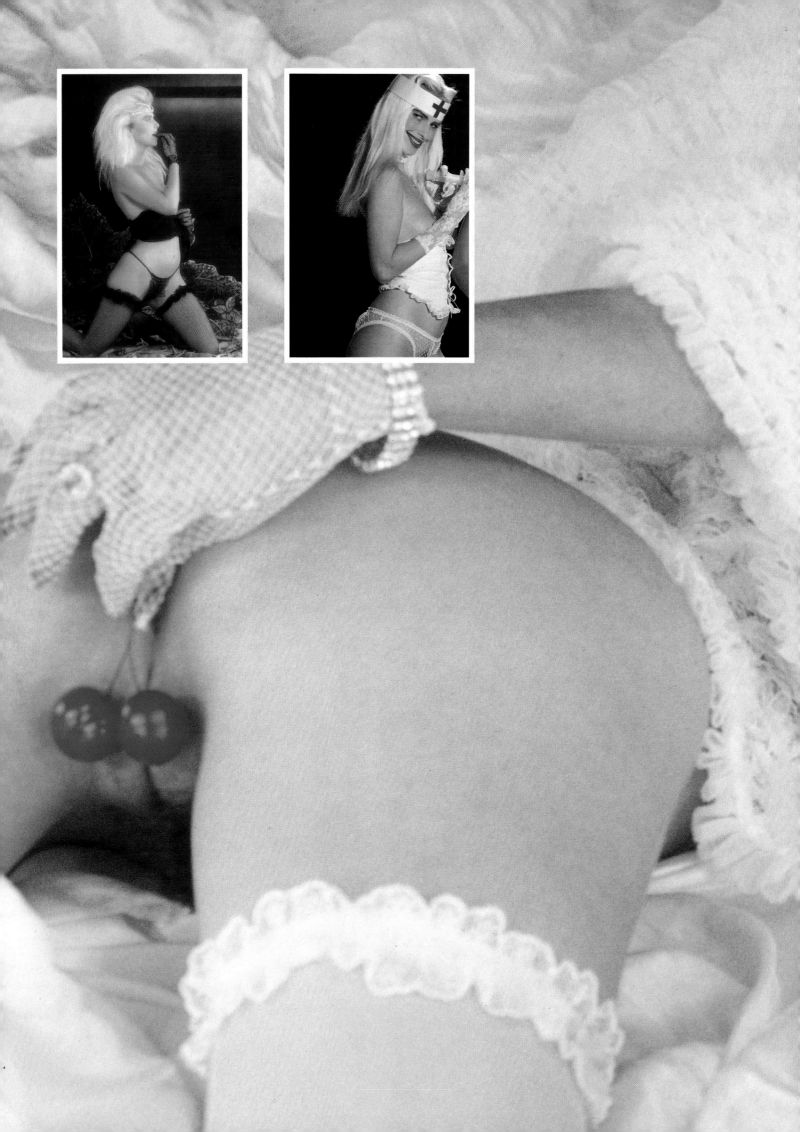

La mia vita è sempre stata un sogno.
Io vivo con grande intensità, perché io amo vivere. Per me la vita è colore, è amore, è sesso, è fantasia, è natura!
Io credo nella sopravvivenza, nell'altra vita! Vorrei che il mio corpo, dopo la mia morte, si trasformi in una farfalla, in un fiore o nel verde!
E chissà che quell'erba verde la mangeranno delle mucche sane, e daranno buon latte, e il latte berranno i buoni bambini!
Ed io sopravvivrò!

Mein Leben war immer ein Traum.
Ich lebe mit großer Intensität, denn ich liebe das Leben.
Das Leben ist für mich Farbe, ist Liebe, Sex, Phantasie, Natur!
Ich glaube an das Weiterleben nach dem Tod! Ich wünsche mir, daß sich mein Körper nach meinem Tod in einen Schmetterling verwandelt – in eine Blume oder in grünes Gras!
Und wer weiß, ob nicht gesunde Kühe dieses grüne Gras fressen und gute Milch geben, und die Milch werden die Kinder trinken!
Und ich werde weiterleben!

My life has always been a dream.
I live life with tremendous intensity, because I love life.
For me, life is colour, love, sex, fantasy, nature!
I believe in life after death. I would like my body to metamorphose into a butterfly after my death – into a flower or into green grass!
And who knows – perhaps healthy cows will eat this green grass and produce fine milk and children will drink the milk!
And I will live on!

Ma vie a toujours été un rêve.
Je vis intensément, car j'aime la vie.
Couleur, amour, sexe, imagination, nature, c'est ça la vie pour moi!
Je crois à la vie après la mort! Je souhaite que mon corps se métamorphose après ma mort en papillon, en fleur ou en herbe verte!
Et qui sait si des vaches resplendissantes de santé ne viendront pas paître cette herbe verte pour donner du bon lait que les enfants boiront!
Et moi, je continuerai à vivre!

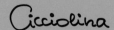

Venezia è una città meravigliosa con le sue gondole, con il suo fascino eterno da favola.
Fare l'amore all'alba nella laguna, con la sua nebbia misteriosa, coi gabbiani bianchi che volano, il vento che ti accarezza con dolcezza è il paradiso terrestre.

Venedig ist eine wunderbare Stadt – mit seinen Gondeln, mit seinem ewigen, märchenhaften Zauber.
Sich bei Sonnenaufgang in der Lagune zu lieben, mit ihrem geheimnisvollen Nebel, mit den weißen Möven, die fliegen, dem Wind, der dich zärtlich liebkost, ist es ein Paradies auf Erden.

Venice is a wonderful city – with its gondolas, and its everlasting, fairytale magic.
Making love on the lagoon at sunrise, with its mystical fog, the white seagulls flying, the wind gently caressing you – this is heaven on earth.

Venise est une ville merveilleuse – avec ses gondoles, son charme éternel et féerique.
S'aimer à l'aurore au bord d'une lagune, avec ses brumes mystérieuses, le vol des mouettes blanches, les tendres caresses du vent, c'est le paradis sur terre.

Cicciolina

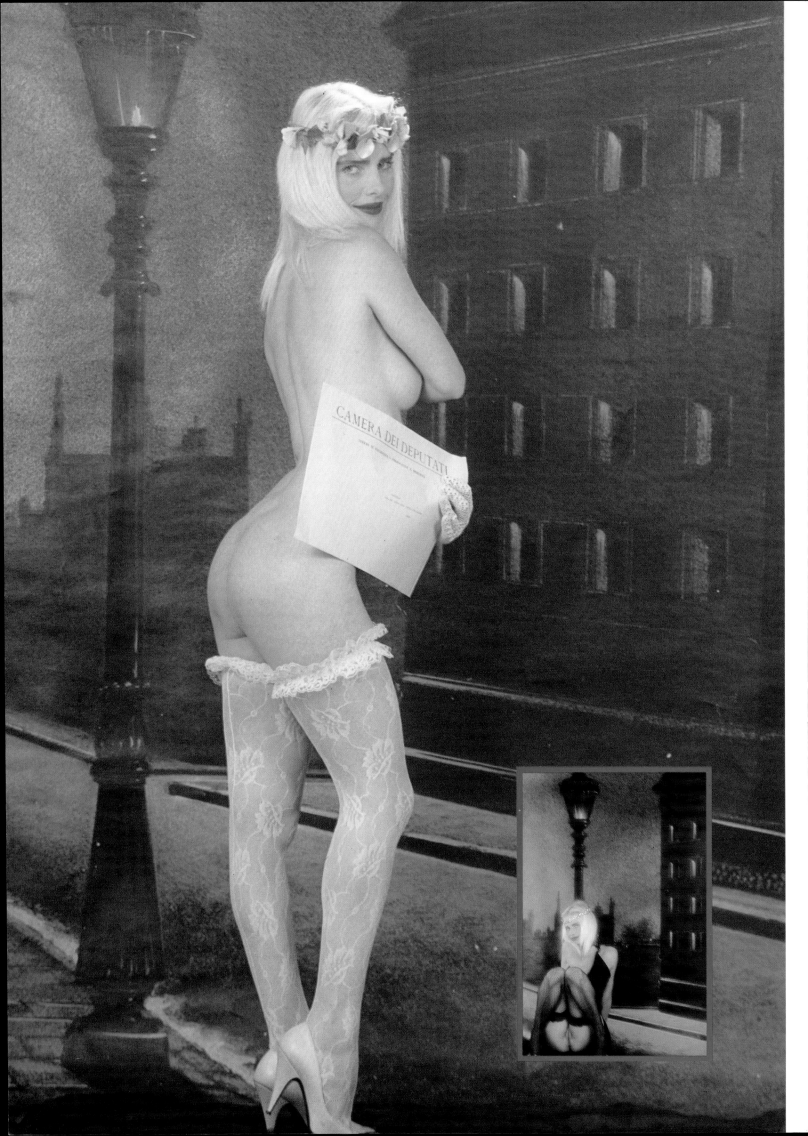

Tutto cambia nella vita!
Cambiano i colori, cambia la gente, cambia l'ideologia dei politici come il colore dei camaleonti.
Prima diventa l'era del fascismo e poi quella del comunismo.
Questa foto è stata scattata a Budapest con l'ultima statua di Lenin (gran simbolo del comunismo).
Con la mia ideologia socialista ho sempre parlato in politica con amore della gente. La mia filosofia sull'amore è viva, come io sono vita!

Alles verändert sich im Leben!
Es ändern sich die Farben, es ändern sich die Menschen, es ändert sich die Ideologie der Politiker wie die Farbe der Chamäleons.
Dieses Photo wurde in Budapest vor der letzten Leninstatue aufgenommen (das Symbol des Kommunismus schlechthin).
Meiner sozialistischen Überzeugung folgend habe ich in der Politik stets mit Liebe von den Belangen der Menschen gesprochen.
Meine Philosophie der Liebe lebt, da ich lebe!

Everything in life changes!
Colours change, people change, political ideologies change like the colours of chameleons.
This photo was taken in Budapest in front of the last statue of Lenin (the ultimate symbol of Communism).
In politics I have always spoken with love about human needs, in line with my Socialist convictions.
My philosophy of love is alive, because I am alive!

La vie n'est que changement!
Les couleurs changent, les hommes changent et l'idéologie des politiciens change comme la couleur du caméléon.
Cette photo a été prise à Budapest, devant la dernière statue de Lénine (le véritable symbole du communisme).
En politique, je suis restée fidèle à mes convictions socialistes et c'est toujours avec amour que j'ai servi la cause des hommes.
Ma philosophie de l'amour est vivante, car je vis!

Cicciolina

In Giappone ho fatto un unico spettacolo per la raccolta di fondi a favore della lotta contro l'AIDS. Ho inoltro incontrato alcuni esponenti del parlamenti giapponese.
In compagnia di studenti giapponesi.

In Japan hatte ich einen einmaligen Auftritt zugunsten der AIDS-Stiftung. Dort traf ich auch mit Politikern des japanischen Parlaments zusammen.
Hier bin ich mit japanischen Schülern zu sehen.

In Japan I did one live performance to raise money for the AIDS foundation.
Here I am with Japanese schoolchildren.

Au Japon, j'ai fait une seule apparition en public au profit de la fondation du SIDA. J'y ai rencontré également des personnalités politiques du parlement japonais.
On peut me voir ici avec des écoliers japonais.

Cicciolina